· LESLIE NIELSEN'S ·
Stupid Little Golf Book

ALSO BY HENRY BEARD

Mulligan's Laws of Golf
The Official Exceptions to the Rules of Golf
Latin For All Occasions
Latin For Even More Occasions

with John Boswell

French For Cats
Advanced French For Exceptional Cats

with Christopher Cerf

The Official Politically Correct Dictionary and Handbook
Sex and Dating: The Official Politically Correct Guide

LESLIE NIELSEN'S
• *Stupid Little Golf Book* •

Leslie Nielsen
&
Henry Beard

HarperCollins*Publishers*

Leslie Nielsen's Bad Golf My Way and
Leslie Nielsen's Bad Golf Made Easier videos
are available from PolyGram Video.

HarperCollins*Publishers*
77–85 Fulham Palace Road,
Hammersmith, London W6 8JB

Published by HarperCollins*Publishers* 1995
1 3 5 7 9 8 6 4 2

A catalogue record for this book is
available from the British Library

ISBN 0 00 638683 0

Set in Bembo

Printed and bound by Scotprint Ltd, Musselburgh, Scotland

• LESLIE NIELSEN'S •
Stupid Little Golf Book

· First Things First, ·
and Vice Versa

Before we get started, I want to make one thing very clear.

I'm not a teacher of golf—or of anything else for that matter.

Yes, I've been called the Duffers' Guru, the High Priest of the High Handicappers, the Bobby Jones of Bad Golf, but I prefer to think of myself as a lifelong student of the game who happened to get a look at a few of the answers when the real teachers left the class to go peek through the window of the girls' locker room.

Now, I'm not saying that golf can't be taught. Golf can be taught.

It's just that it can't be learned.

This fundamental and unalterable fact explains why so many aspiring players spend so much time and money taking lessons from gifted instructors and never seem to improve. In fact, they usually get worse.

Of course, that doesn't explain how so many pros can still make a living teaching it, but then, there's a lot about golf I don't understand.

People always told me, if I took everything I didn't know about the game, it would fill a book.

Well, I guess they were right.

· A LITTLE CAREER ·
GUIDANCE

Some years back I was playing in a pro-am charity event in the Midwest, and a tousle-haired youngster came up to me as I was hitting balls on the range.

"Mr. Nielsen," he stammered nervously, "I hate to bother you, but I'm trying to decide whether to become a golfer or an actor."

I gave him my driver. "Hit a couple of balls," I said.

He set up and cracked a pair of 275-yard boomers in a row, straight as an arrow.

I reached into my bag and pulled out a rolled-up film script I planned to read when play got slow, which it always does in these tournaments. I opened it to a page with a pretty long speech on it and handed it to him.

"All right," I said, "take a crack at this."

He looked confused for a moment, then stood the

script up on its end, took a big swing, and whacked it.

He hit that damn thing so hard, the club just crushed it to a pulp, but it went way right and only about fifty yards.

"Son," I said, "I think you should stick to golf."

And do you know where that young man is today?

Neither do I.

· THE GRIP ·

Golfers were always worrying about, and fiddling with, their grips.

Is my grip too strong or too weak? Should the "V"s formed by my thumbs and forefingers point to my chin or my right shoulder? Is my hand pressure too tight? Are the calluses on my palm in the right place?

The way I see it, the grip is the simplest thing to master in the game of golf.

There is only one absolutely inflexible rule you must follow when you take your grip. Obey it, and you will have eliminated from your game forever some of the most god-awful shots you could possibly imagine.

Here it is: Always hold the club at the thin end where that length of rubber stuff is, and not the end that has that curvy metal or wooden thing with the number on it.

Now, if you don't think that one piece of advice is worth the whole price of this book, just go ahead and try hitting a couple of buckets of balls holding the club the other way around.

· THE STANCE ·

A good stance is a key part of golf.

Address the ball. Square up the club. Now drop your head slightly until the ground between your legs comes into sight.

You should see two feet. If you don't see any feet, or only one foot, or three or more feet, you need to work on your stance.

· What Do You See? ·

Which part of the ball do you focus on when you swing?

Some books tell you to look at the back of the ball or the inside quarter.

I believe that to promote clean contact, your eyes should be on the bottom of the ball.

When you set up to hit, if you can't see the lower half of the ball because it's sitting down in the rough or in a divot or hollow in the fairway, take the time to roll it over onto a tuft of grass until at least some of the underside comes into view.

It's a small thing, but I've often found that in golf, if you pay attention to the little details, the big problems take care of themselves.

· LOOKING UP ·

If you ask a golfer what he thinks caused the bad shot he just hit, he'll almost always say, "I looked up."

Now, all the golf books by famous players and successful teachers claim that looking up isn't really the cause of the mishit; it's just another symptom of the swing error that was the real culprit. And they all say that you have to correct that error in order to keep your head steady, and not the other way around.

I happen to disagree.

I believe that the *only* thing you actually have to do to play decent golf is to keep your head still when you swing, which is, unfortunately, just about impossible.

I also believe that the only thing that separates good golfers from bad golfers is that good golfers always keep their heads still, and always have, and they simply can't imagine what it's like to move their heads when they swing, any more than we can imagine not being happy with a seventy-nine.

I am not going to mislead you. I do not have the secret of keeping your head still. But I'm happy to share with you a few swing thoughts that have been of absolutely no use whatsoever is keeping my own head still, but which I have employed with some success in an effort to get opponents to start lifting theirs.

- You are standing on the surface of Jupiter. To raise your head would require a superhuman effort. In fact, the gravity is so intense, the snot in your nose weighs more than a pickup truck.

- You have inadvertently shampooed with nitroglycerin. If you move your noggin so much as a fraction of an inch, you're going to have to take a fairly lengthy cab ride to scratch your ear.

- The deadly death's-head spider has landed on your shirt collar. Though no larger than the period at the end of the previous sentence, this skittish and ill-tempered insect secretes a venom so poisonous that a single drop in an urban reservoir system could fell a circus elephant fed just one peanut held briefly in the fingers of a visitor to the big top who shook hands earlier that day with a man who had washed in that city's water supply one week earlier.

• Carlos, the notorious international terrorist, stands at the end of the tee. If you look up, he will assume that you will be able to provide a description of his much-altered appearance to the police forces of the sixteen nations who have hunted this vicious killer code-named "the Jackal" for two decades. Yes, his AK-47 will make a deafening racket bound to attract the attention of other players on the course as the high-powered slugs explode from the barrel of his machine pistol and turn you into just so much zarzuela de carne (the spicy Venezuelan meat stew that has been his favorite dish since boyhood), but, really, what choice does he have?

· JUST FOR BEGINNERS ·

People often ask me what I would tell someone taking up the game of golf for the first time. Do I have a few brief insights I could convey to a beginner about to embark on what could well be a lifelong quest to master the world's most challenging pastime?

Well, I've given that question a lot of thought over the years, pondering how I could distill the essence of the game into a couple of well-chosen phrases that would get a new student off on the right foot, and after much reflection and soul-searching, I guess I'd say just three simple things:

- There's no charge for using the ball washers.
- The carts make a funny noise when you put them in reverse.
- The little pencils are free.

· DON'T THINK ·

The swing key that helps you hit the ball solidly to-day can turn you into a hopeless hacker tomorrow, but there is one thought I've found that always works.

That thought is, Don't Think.

You must never forget not to think. But you can't just forget not to think—you must remember not to remember to think, and you must not remember that you forgot to think.

I'll admit that's a lot to not think about out there on the golf course, but even if you sometimes forget not to forget not to think about your swing, you can certainly see to it that your opponent remembers to remember to think about his.

· THE FIRST ·
FUNDAMENTAL

Ask any player what he thinks is the first fundamental of the game of golf, and he'll probably say the Vardon Grip.

For me, it's the Vardon *Tip*—the little sweetener you put in the hands of the starter to get you off in front of a bunch of slow foursomes lined up waiting to go out.

Fold a twenty-dollar bill over twice and slip it into the center of your right hand. Let your fingers close over it lightly, bending them into a loose fist.

Approach the starter and shake his hand firmly— not a bone-crusher, just good solid palm-to-palm contact.

As you feel the bill being taken, make a good release, and pull your hand straight back.

Then head right out to the first tee: You're up next!

· DON'T PRACTICE LONGER · —PRACTICE SMARTER

I see players out on the driving range every day, banging bucket after bucket of balls, or lagging dozens of twenty-footers on the putting green, or whomping shovelfuls of sand out of the practice bunker. And then I see the same players glumly forking over their cash at the end of the round. Did they end up three down after two presses because they didn't practice enough? No, it's because they practiced the wrong things.

Now, I'm not saying that you shouldn't warm up properly before a round of golf. I generally get the kinks out by blading a dozen or so balls with an old 2-iron. Not only does swinging the horrible thing make every club in my bag look and feel as easy to hit as a wedge, but warming up with it while the rest of my foursome watches greatly strengthens my claim to an eighteen handicap.

But my real practice is over long before I get to the course. Here are just a couple of drills from my basic routine.

A few times a month I go to a miniature golf course and play a round without a putter, using only my foot to kick the ball. I may not be able to hoe a hooded 4-iron out from under a bush, or dig a wedge out of a hollow in the deep rough, or slap a backhanded 8-iron off a tree root, but it's amazing how rarely I actually end up having to hit my ball out of a lie as bad as that.

Here's another stroke-saving exercise I've made part of my regular program.

I practice "shooting" the ball at the hole with my thumb and forefinger, just the way you used to do in a childhood game of marbles.

You'd be surprised how many scary ten-footers you can turn into makable tap-ins if you'll take those few extra minutes a day to polish up your ball-marking skills.

· WHICH CLUB? ·

It's remarkable how often a fellow golfer will ask you what club you think he should use for his next shot.

I want to say, look, how the hell should I know, when I can barely figure out what I, with whose game I am somewhat more familiar, should hit, but that's a little rude. So here's what I do instead.

I say listen, it's simple.

Figure out the yardage from the nearest sprinkler head or marker or from the yardage book. Okay, 195 yards.

Drop the last digit and divide by 2. If there's a remainder, just drop that too. That leaves 9.

Now, subtract the number of strokes you've already taken on the hole. Let's say you lie 2, so we get 7.

All right, now multiply your handicap by your hat size. We'll say you're a 14.3 (forget the part right of the decimal) and you wear a 6⅞ (forget the fraction). Six times 14 is 84.

Since that's less than 100, we *add* the par of the hole—we'll assume it's a par 5—to that number we got earlier. Seven plus 5 equals 12.

Hit the 12-iron.

Nobody asks twice.

· ARE YOU SWINGING · HARD ENOUGH?

Bad golfers look at Freddie Couples's slow, deliberate, effortless swing and say to themselves, "Gee, if I could just swing the club like that, I could hit the ball a mile."

That's just plain nonsense. If you get up on the tee and swing that driver as easy as Freddie does, you'll hit the ball fifty-five yards.

The only way the average player can get any distance is by swinging the club as hard as possible, and that total-power "killing" swing starts with a good solid death grip.

Sam Snead said he held the club as lightly as he would if he had a live bird in his hands, but I want you to grab that thing as if you were throttling a poisonous snake or trying to squeeze one last bit of toothpaste out of a crowbar.

To initiate your swing, clench your teeth in a firm

"jaw press" and then pull the club sharply up. A good way to visualize this critical early part of the "takeway" is to imagine you're whisking a tablecloth out from under an elaborately set-up banquet table. It doesn't matter if all the china and glasses end up on the floor—you just want a nice, fast tugging motion that gets the club headed back in a hurry.

The key to really powdering the ball is starting your downswing as early in your backswing as you can—preferably before the club gets much farther than waist high, and long before it has been raised into the power-robbing "busboy" position way up around your head.

A lot of golfers say to themselves "One-and-*two*" to get a sense of when to trigger the downswing. This is crazy. If you've got to count, just say *"Two!"* and smack the ball.

The swinging motion you're after is somewhere between that long, lateral move the guy makes when he rings the gong at the beginning of J. Arthur Rank films and the forceful body-powered chopping stroke you'd use if you were demolishing a cinder-block wall with a sledgehammer.

How can you tell if you've really gotten every last ounce of oomph at your command into the shot? Ideally, one or both of your feet should come out of your shoes, your club shaft should bounce sharply off your shoulder (I like to see a callus there), and your watch should stop.

You aren't overswinging unless the club actually flies out of your hand (except on the drive, where this is normal), or the head comes off, or you finish your follow-through on your hands and knees (unless it's a long iron, in which case this position is okay).

I know what you're going to say. Why doesn't Freddie Couples swing hard and *really* crush the ball? Well, think about it. What is the use of a 725-yard drive on a 390-yard par-4?

· PLAYING IN THE WIND ·

Nothing wrecks a bad golfer's game faster than a windy day. I don't care if it's a flag-snapping three-club gale or a leaf-pounding one-sixteenth of a club howling breeze. If you want to shoot a halfway decent score, you've got to do something to compensate for the manifest unfair playing conditions.

Probably the simplest adjustment you can make is to subtract the apparent average wind speed from your final score. Thus, if you shot, say, a 135 and the wind, at a conservative estimate, was blowing 56 mph, you'd shoot a quite respectable 79.

Another option I'd recommend if the windy conditions have pretty much emptied out the course is to pick a nice, straight not-too-long par-4 where the wind is directly behind you the whole way, and play it eighteen times.

A third alternative is to figure out how many extra clubs you have to take on any hole where the wind is in your face, and simply subtract that number of strokes from your score, but considering the commendably aggressive stroke-tabulating methods employed by many bad golfers, this approach can lead to the potential scorekeeping nightmare of completing a hole in minus numbers.

· CAVEAT GOLFOR ·

When you take a brand-new ball out of a sleeve on the tee of a hole, I really think you're entitled to a "test drive."

If it turns out to be a lemon—usually because there's something wrong with the steering or the brakes—then I'd just leave it "parked" in the water hazard or the woods or wherever it ended up and try another. No penalty.

This applies to a used ball too, so long as you just got it out of the bowl in the pro shop, and this is the first time you've taken it out "for a spin."

But I draw the line at range balls. You deserve what you get if you choose to go around your local track with something that's been in the golfing equivalent of a demolition derby.

· THE RIGHT ELBOW ·

Is the right elbow important in golf?

I would say very definitely yes, unless you plan to always ask for a straw, or you're a southpaw and you're used to holding your drink in your left hand.

· WANNA BET? ·

Betting is a big part of the game of golf, but I've never seen much point to it. I think the only time you should gamble is in a game that has some element of skill in it, like blackjack or craps or poker, and golf, at least for bad golfers, is clearly not a game of skill.

Golfers often say they bet "just to put some fun in the game," but I've found that having even small amounts of money at stake makes players nitpick endlessly over minor details of the rules, like penalty strokes and whether you get a free throw from behind a tree and when it's okay to rake the ball out of the trap, and for me that takes the fun *out* of the game.

Nevertheless, there are times when, out of simple politeness, you have to go along with a "friendly" $5 Nassau with $2 "trash" bets on things like Sandies and Greenies, and when that happens, I suggest that you propose some additional $2 "bad golfer" side bets to keep your head above water. Rattle them off in a hurry, and try not to explain exactly what they are.

Here are a few of my favorites.

- Booties—nicest shoes (check out the competing footgear before including this one)
- Weenies—shortest drive
- Whoopsies—ball closest to center of next fairway
- Fwangies—strangest-sounding iron shot
- Topsies—shortest fairway wood
- Turfies—biggest divot
- Greedies—most ridiculous shot
- Obies—farthest Out of Bounds
- Uglies—most successful missed shot
- Hurlies—longest club toss
- Handies—ball thrown closest to pin
- Takies—longest uncontested picked-up putt
- Wheelies—fastest to next hole
- Washies—first to get to the ball washer on the next tee

· Cut Those Long · Putts Down to Size

The next time you line up a thirty-foot putt, look at it this way: It's simply ten three-footers laid end to end.

Even if you leave that monster putt short, you just sank eight or nine short putts in a row without giving it a second thought.

· The Lesson Tee ·

If you've played golf for any time at all, you know by now that taking a lesson is the quickest and surest way to ruin your game.

The trouble is, every now and then the fatal urge to improve becomes too much for you to resist, and before you know what happened, you're out there on the lesson tee.

There you stand, resting fifty-five percent of your weight on your right foot and forty-five percent on your left foot, with a strap wrapped around your elbows and a hanky tucked in your right armpit, staring in a baffled daze at the weird lines and arrows spray-painted in the grass, getting ready to hit the back inside quarter of a golf ball with a 7-iron held in a grip more suited for a pipe wrench.

Suddenly, the full horror of what you have brought down upon yourself dawns on you.

You are about to have the wheels removed from

your game swiftly and efficiently by a trained professional wielding a high-speed air-driven lug wrench. The hubcaps are already off, and if you don't do something in a hurry, you're going to have a long journey back from utter destruction to mere mediocrity.

I'll be honest with you. There is no way to totally eliminate the harmful effects of one-on-one golf instruction. Not even the most devious and inspired competitor wielding the subtlest needle can get your game off its rails faster than a dedicated P.G.A. pro determined to get your clubface square at the top, your weight properly shifted to the insides of your feet, and your swing on plane from take-away to follow-through.

It isn't easy to maintain your confidence in your own deeply flawed, tried-and-true method of swinging the club in the face of an onslaught of clearly appropriate but totally devastating corrections and modifications offered by a well-meaning zealot, but there are a few self-defense measures you can take.

—Ask your instructor to make a few swings. See if you can find something he does differently from the top pros. If you spot some small thing, point it out to him. (He'll appreciate the tip!)

—Ask him if he knows how to make that neat shot from a steep downhill lie on the back wall of a bunker where you hit the ball backward over your own head. If he does, make him show you. If he doesn't, look surprised and disappointed.

—To use up time, get him to teach you those little moves the pros all make before they hit a shot, where they twirl the club in their hands and tug at the collar of their polo shirts.

—Tell him the pro at the resort where you go in the winter can hold a wedge in his right hand and bounce a ball fifty times in a row off its face without stopping. Look expectant.

—If he starts to give you any actual instruction, try to picture him as Bozo the Clown. Visualize the dopey red nose, the silly clown suit, and the big floppy shoes.

—Ask him if he always dreamed of being a teaching pro, or whether he had some other ambition.

—If all else fails, ask him to deliberately shank a few balls, just so you can see what really causes it.

· WINTER RULES ·

I agree wholeheartedly with the custom of letting golfers improve their lies when winter weather makes play difficult.

However, I do think it's a mistake to limit the time when "preferred lies" are permitted to the period from November through March.

Let's not forget that not so very long ago, most of modern-day North America and Europe was under about a mile of ice for several thousand years. By the time the glaciers finally retreated, they had really chewed up the landspace, leaving behind all sorts of hollows, hummocks, hogbacks, saddles, swales, knolls, ravines, slopes, and other types of uphill, downhill, and sidehill lies that golfers have to contend with to this day.

Therefore, I think that since the unfavorable

playing conditions created by the severe and prolonged "winter" of the last Ice Age are still very much with us, golfers should be entitled to roll the ball over, or, in extreme cases, tee it up, 365 days a year.

· A RAW DEAL ·

Everybody thinks left-handed players get a raw deal in golf, and at first glance it looks like they have a point.

Left-handed sets of clubs cost more and are harder to find than regular clubs, and pro shops usually stock only a few sizes of right-hand gloves.

The way most courses are designed, lefties always seem to get a bad break. If they slice, they slice, and if they hit a nice draw, that's a slice too, because the ball ends up in a bunker or a big fat bush or something the architect put there to catch a right-hander's slice.

And it's hard enough to figure out what's wrong with your swing when right from the very beginning you're doing everything backward.

But there's another side to the story. Southpaws can hit those neat left-handed shots when they're stymied behind a tree and someone is watching, and when you think about it, even the worst shot they hit is a helluva trick shot, and if you don't believe me, try hitting any kind of shot at all with a left-handed 5-iron.

If they leave a wedge on the green, they're probably going to get it back, and they can see at a glance that the latest $25 illustrated golf book with a revolutionary new swing secret is of absolutely no use to them without having to buy and read the damn thing.

And maybe best of all, when some guy whom you just saw sneeze into his mitt recognizes you out on the course and comes over to shake your hand, what do you know?

There's a glove on it.

· LUCK ·

There are two kinds of luck in golf, dumb luck and smart luck.

It's dumb luck if by some accident you hit a drive in the absolute center of the club and the ball goes straight as an arrow 240 yards right down the middle of the fairway.

It's smart luck if you hit a drive way out of bounds, but fortune lends a hand, and in a remarkable turn of events, you find your ball a good thirty yards inside the O.B. line, sitting up on a nice tuft of grass with a clear shot to the green.

· THE OUTER GAME ·
OF GOLF

Everyone agrees that golf is a mental game. The trouble is that your mind is difficult to control because you have to control it with your mind, and there's no way to keep your mind from figuring out what's going on.

You can, however, control your opponent's mind with carefully timed comments at key moments during a match.

Now, the "needle," as these deadly little pointed observations are collectively known, wasn't exactly invented yesterday, so really old standbys like "What do you think about when you start your downswing?" or "Gosh, you've certainly been keeping your head steady lately" have been rendered largely ineffective through overuse.

Here are a few fresher phrases that I have employed with some success recently. Of course, as they become more widely known, their impact will necessarily be reduced, but I believe that early purchasers of this valuable volume should be richly rewarded for their commendable display of foresight and taste:

- You've never been here in 2 before.
- Did you watch that L.P.G.A. tournament last week? You can't believe how far some of those women can hit the ball.
- Hey, you know who does that same loop thing that you do at the top of your swing? Nancy Lopez.
- Looks like I'm pretty much out of the hole. All you have to do to win is keep the ball in play.
- I'll stand right behind you and watch your shot —you keep your eyes glued on that ball.
- Daly had a shot just like that in the U.S. Open and he put it stiff to the pin with an *8-iron*.
- Have you ever seen a picture of what's inside your knee?
- Wow, what a great lie! I guess you can go ahead and hit the driver right off the fairway.

· The Importance · of Footwork

I hesitate to argue with top teaching pros like Peter Kostis, Bob Toski, and David Leadbetter, but one criticism they make about bad golfers I disagree with one hundred percent, and that is their oft-voiced observation that less-accomplished players rarely use their feet effectively.

Whether we're nonchalantly stepping on an unscrupulous opponent's ball in the rough, or getting ourselves out of trouble and into a decent lie with a subtle "come-along" toe flick or a deft backward "roll and go" brush with the bottom of the shoe, I think bad golfers display some of the soundest footwork you'll see in the game.

But I would add a few words of warning for those of my fellow high-handicappers who sometimes get a little carried away with their pedal prowess.

Don't tread a competitor's ball so heavily that it sticks to one of your spikes.

Don't drop-kick your ball or put it up on a tee and take a punt-style run at it.

And if you have to take off your shoes and socks and roll up your pants to reach it, kicking a ball out of a water hazard is really not a viable option.

· GO FIGURE ·

A wise man (it may have been me) once said that the game of golf is larger than anything you can carry it around in—something is always sticking out.

If you can drive, and hit your irons decently, you won't be able to putt.

And if you can sink everything in sight, your sand game will go south, and you'll top every fairway wood.

There is some point to all of this, but I can't for the life of me think of what it is.

· The Eight Bad Shots · of Golf and How to Make Them Work for You

All golfers everywhere are always hoping for that absolutely perfect shot hit dead in the center of the sweet spot, and they keep trying to "swing in the barrel" or "toll the bell" to get it. Alas, when they finally do make pure flawless contact with that 4-iron or that fairway wood, most of the time they end up in trouble, either because the ball flew straight as an arrow into the woods when they were allowing for a slice, or it soared forty yards farther than they ever dreamed possible and knocked someone cold on the apron of the green.

The truth is, it makes much more sense to go for a dependable miss than run the risk of suddenly hitting a miraculous shot into outer space. And if an attempt to hit a dead solid perfect shot produces a less than miraculous result that still does something unpredictable, like actually hooking for once, you can find yourself wasting a lot of strokes.

To put it another way, a good *bad* shot is almost always better than a bad *good* shot.

With that in mind, you should take the time to get good at golf's bad shots. Yes, there are hundreds of them, but eight of them are the basic bread-and-butter boo-boos of great bad golfers:

1. The Sliced Drive. Aim way left, take a fast, short backswing, and spin your hips into the ball, making sure that you are already looking down the fairway before the club makes contact. Swing Thought: "Beat the Clock." Purpose of the Shot: To take all the trouble on the left side of the hole completely out of play. The ball goes right toward the condominium, then suddenly curves back and comes into the fairway at right angles.

2. The Skied Drive. Lift the club sharply upward on the backswing, shift your weight to your left side, then sway into the ball with your hands

well ahead of the club. Swing Thought: "Whomp the Rug." Purpose of the Shot: To guarantee that the ball will end up in the middle of a narrow tricky fairway, even if it's only one hundred yards out. Much more reliable—and much less embarrassing—than hitting a wedge off the tee of a par-4 or par-5.

3. Topped Fairway Wood. Swing your whole body back with the club, then as you swing down, straighten your right knee, put all your weight on your right foot, and lift your shoulders. Swing Thought: "Kick the Puppy." Purpose of the Shot: Reliable, straight shot that whizzes along the ground and never goes farther than 125 yards no matter how hard it is hit. Ideal for layups.

4. Shanked Iron. Stand close to the ball and make a quick wristy swing with as little pivot as possible. Swing Thought: "Crack the Whip." Purpose of the Shot: To hit a ball around a tree when opponents are standing too close to per-

mit a minor lie adjustment; also, to discourage opponents from standing too close to permit a minor lie adjustment. The ball rockets off to the right at a 45- to 90-degree angle, approximately head high.

5. Sclaffed Medium Iron. Bend the left knee, dip the left shoulder, and throw the club head at the ball from the top. Swing Thought: "Pound the Mole." Purpose of the Shot: To permit the player to use his favorite 7-iron even though it is only ninety yards to the green. The shot cannot be skulled, and the huge divot absorbs excess club-head energy; the ball goes straight, and rolls softly onto the green.

6. Bladed Wedge. Hold the club extra tight at the start of the swing to promote a loosening of the grip at the top; raise right elbow and bend left arm, then swing out, around, down, and over. Swing Thought: "Choke the Chicken." Purpose of the Shot: To give the ball enough piz-

zazz to skip a dozen or more times across a water hazard or run through a bunker.

7. Chippitch or Pitchip. Stand away from the ball, shift your weight to your right foot, lock your knees, tighten your elbows, and a make a jerky, loose-wristed swing that keeps your hands behind the ball. Swing Thought: "Smother the Bug." Purpose of the Shot: To take the guesswork out of whether to chip or pitch the ball by always making an indecisive, poorly timed "halfway" shot. The ball never goes straight up and lands short, and even if it is hit thin, it has too little power to sail over the green.

8. The Stubbed Putt. Use any putting style you prefer, but lift your head up to look at the hole before the putter strikes the ball and make a short, jabbing stroke, primarily with the wrists. Begin walking briskly after the putt and pick it up as soon as it begins to slow down no matter how far it is from the hole. Swing Thought:

"Pick the Daisy." Purpose of the Shot: To make a weakly hit, slow-moving putt that can be easily intercepted and picked up as a "gimme" before it has a chance to stop rolling, thus guaranteeing a two-putt.

· A FOOLPROOF WAY TO ·
KNOCK AT LEAST SIX
STROKES OFF YOUR SCORE

Skip the last hole.

· CASUAL TIMBER ·

There's an old saying that trees are ninety percent air, but every time I've tried to hit through one, it has seemed to me that if those proportions are indeed correct, there's been some misunderstanding all these years, and what we've been breathing is actually called "wood."

But what golfers often forget is that trees, like many other living things, really and truly are ninety percent *water*.

Now, as far as I'm concerned, quibbling over that last ten percent is just hairsplitting. It may look like a solid oak, but if ninety percent of that thing standing between you and the green is water, it's water, period, or, to be more exact, it's "a temporary accumulation of water visible to the player when he takes his stance," which, of course, is the definition in the Rules of Casual Water.

Obviously it's temporary, because no tree lives

forever, and it certainly is visible when you take your stance, so you're allowed a free drop. Two club lengths away is the distance you get in the casual water rule, but considering the extreme nature of the obstruction, and the difficulty in determining precisely where it begins and ends, what with all the roots and branches, I really think one tree-length away is fairer.

· ADDRESSING THE BALL ·
IN THE FAIRWAY

Most golfers use some variation of the waggle, a little back-and-forth wave of the club, usually followed by a forward press of their hands or hips, as a reliable, repeatable way to initiate their swings.

I've found that a couple of superficially similar but far more effective motions are a much better way to "get the ball rolling."

The first is the cudgel, which is nothing more than a few sharp up-and-down thumps in back of the ball with a fairway wood.

The second is a solid, shaft-bending *downward* press or push with the head of the club soled right behind the ball.

Both of these simple movements help to promote

the feeling that you're going to make solid contact with the dead center of the ball, and they serve to eliminate that nagging tension caused by having to hit out of a tight or cuppy lie in the fairway or the light rough.

· THE IDEAL FOURSOME ·

I suppose every player dreams of playing a round of golf in a foursome with some of the game's all-time greats.

You, Arnold Palmer, Sam Snead, and Ben Hogan, or you, Jack Nicklaus, Gary Player, and Tom Watson.

It would certainly be an incredible honor to play with these legendary golfers, but let's face it, they all take the game very seriously, and they all have a pretty uncompromising attitude when it comes to the rules.

That's why when you get right down to it, if I had an opportunity to play with a trio of really outstanding individuals, but still wanted to have some fun and stand a chance of turning in a decent scorecard, I'd pick George Shearing, Ray Charles, and Stevie Wonder.

· Tools of the Trade ·

If you ask a pro or a scratch amateur golfer what the most important clubs in the bag are, you'll always get the same answer: the driver, the putter, and the wedge.

That may be true for the more accomplished player, but as far as bad golfers are concerned, the only things that you can really count on aren't in your bag at all.

- Your "hand wedge" or "five-fingered iron," because when your ball is in a footprint in a bunker, or deep in the woods, there is no such thing as using "too much right hand."

- The old reliable leather-topped 8 or 9 or 10½ EEE that's always right there when you need it, because when your ball is stymied or sitting down in a rotten lie, you need to really "lace it."

- That trusty #2 wooden pencil, because one single carefully executed stroke of this graphite-filled beauty can knock five shots off your score.

· WHY YOU SHOULD ·
ALWAYS GO FOR IT

Let's say you've hit a pretty good drive on a par-4 with a water hazard in front of the green. Your second shot will have to carry 175 yards in the air to make it to dry land. Do you go for it?

Always. I know that a lot of master golf strategists, like Rebecca De Mornay, are going to disagree with me on this one, but I can prove with absolute mathematical certainty that if you play safe, you're going to be sorry.

Suppose you go for it and your second shot takes a bath. After the penalty stroke you lie 4.

Now, let's say you chicken out and lay up just short of the water. It's one hundred percent certain that you're going to top or blade your third shot. It goes for a swim, and you take the penalty stroke. But now you lie 5.

Of course, in both cases you still have to go over

the water, but I'm feeling a lot more confident with my 4 than Mr. Conservative over there who's starting to roll the second ball into place and is staring at an 8.

He's also staring at an instant replay of the shot he just booted into the drink, while I'm looking at a little no-sweat wedge that's a piece of cake compared to that 3-iron with a 175-yard forced carry I just hit.

I also have a very good lie from the deft ball drop I made while he was concentrating on hitting his third shot, but that's another story.

· Mr. Know-It-All ·

Sooner or later you will run into the most obnoxious individual on any golf course: the normally mediocre player who through some total fluke is playing wonderful golf and is eager to share with you the secret of the game, which he has had the enormous good fortune to have stumbled upon.

He can't wait to tell you how hitting against a strong left side, or pronating his wrists, or initiating his swing with his right shoulder has absolutely transformed his game, and he will jump at the chance to point out any flaws in your style of play.

There is only one way to handle this smug jerk: with an immediate full-bore counterattack.

Tell him that while your game is a little off right now, what has really worked for you in the past is trying to pull against a "heavy pinky" with your left hand in your take-away, and feeling that your wrists are "wet" in the backswing. Add that at the top you always think "sticky toes," at impact you want your armpits to seem "empty," and you always concentrate on maintaining "sharp knuckles" during your follow-through.

Explain that several drills have helped you recently: swinging with your wrists manacled in an ordinary pair of police handcuffs and a child's balloon tied to your right elbow; gripping carrots hard enough to puree them through your fingers; hitting hard-boiled eggs off a tee with a 1-iron; and practicing putting down a flight of stairs into a dustpan.

Share with him your favorite swing thoughts: imagining that you're standing barefoot on a bed of hot coals to develop "lively feet"; visualizing that you're turning your jaw away from a dentist's drill as you begin your swing; and thinking of yourself at the top, perfectly aligned along a set of railroad tracks down which a locomotive is barreling at high speed.

When he starts to get a little glassy-eyed, show him what *he's* doing wrong. Make a swing and stop it at the top. Say, "This is how you're swinging." Then

make an *absolutely identical* swing and say, "This is the
way Hogan did it—see the difference?"

Finally, as a last lethal salvo, let him in on a few of
these one hundred percent fatal memory aids:

- Grip with fists, twist the wrists
- Shift the weight, don't hit late
- Shorter pivot, better divot
- Shift those feet, hit it sweet
- Bad lie, swing hands high
- Afraid of trees? Freeze those knees!
- Ball in rough—is club enough?
- Ball in sand, call in hands
- Short chips, "hula" the hips
- To make ball stop, swing from top
- To stop that shank, keep mind blank

· A USEFUL TIP ·

I find it helpful to inform an opponent who is lining up a four-foot putt that under the metric system widely used in other countries, it's actually a putt of just over 1,200 millimeters.

· HANDICAPS ·

Handicaps are a wonderful invention that lets players of widely differing skills compete on an equal basis, but, useful as they are, they do suffer from an unfortunate rigidity.

This lack of flexibility is due to the fact that the calculation of a golfer's handicap is based entirely on a statistical averaging of his scores on a handful of rounds played under normal conditions over a period of many weeks or months.

The simple one- or two-digit number produced by this mechanical computation is fine as far as it goes, but it fails to take into account the injuries, misfortunes, and other complications and special circumstances that may negatively affect a golfer's playing ability on any particular day.

For this reason, I recommend the adoption of my Temporary Mishap Adjustment Index. The beauty of this eminently fair plan is that additional handicap strokes are automatically awarded to players based on a Universal Adversity Scale, thereby eliminating the acrimonious, game-delaying discussions and negotiations that golfers currently engage in on the first tee.

I'm presently putting the finishing touches on the Nielsen Stroke-Equalization System (I'm still tinkering with some of the Impairment Severity Ratings), but here's an idea of how it works:

- Hangnail, bad haircut—add one stroke
- Dandruff, chapped lips, excess ear-wax build-up, uncomfortable underwear, piece of food caught between teeth—add two strokes
- Blister, scratch, cut, or Band-Aid on either hand; bruised knuckles; lost dry cleaning—add three strokes
- Headache, upset stomach, mild cold or flu symptoms, new shoes, old glove (if no replacement is available at a reasonable cost in pro shop) —add five strokes
- Recent weight gain, new glasses, car in shop— add eight strokes

- Hangover, upcoming medical appointment, recent death of pet—add ten strokes
- New clubs, knee brace or tennis-elbow strap worn on any limb, read golf book within previous week (must have book in question in possession)—add twelve strokes
- Back pain, sore shoulder, pulled muscle, sprained ankle, stiff neck, arrived too late to hit balls on the range, just met daughter's new boyfriend (past forty-eight hours)—add fifteen strokes
- Severe toothache, cast on either foot, recent bad sex (last night)—add eighteen strokes
- Marital or financial difficulties, operation within past month or scheduled for next month, formal golf lesson within previous week—add twenty strokes

· THE ALL-TIME LEADER · IN PENALTY STROKES

When your club head hits the ground behind the ball, and the only thing you get airborne is a huge divot, do you have to count the shot?

The answer to that question is simple and straightforward: If the ball moves, you must add a stroke to your score.

On the other hand, if only the earth moves, then the earth—which is also a ball, albeit a very large one —is assessed the stroke.

Incidentally, as of last count, our home planet lies 1,735,962,044,288,391.

· HOW TO PLAY YOUR ·
BEST BAD GOLF

Someone (I think it was either Jean-Paul Sartre or Fabian) once asked me what was the greatest golf shot I ever saw.

I didn't have to stop to think. It was a four-inch putt that Humphrey Bogart missed on the eighteenth at Riviera. The ball lipped out, and he ended up one-down to the head of Columbia Pictures, who was trying to decide whether to give the role of Captain Queeg in *The Caine Mutiny* to Bogart, who really wanted it, or to his own first choice, Gene Autry.

I asked him about that putt sometime later, and Bogie (a dumb nickname, since he was a scratch golfer) told me the only harder shot he ever had to make was when he hit a ball out of Peter Lorre's ear in the famous driving-range scene that was cut from *Casablanca*.

I told him I believed it. As difficult as it is to play even so-so golf on any given day, there is no more demanding challenge facing even the worst golfer than playing consistently reliable and believable terrible golf on purpose.

It looks like it ought to be the easiest thing in the world, but when you think about it, there are two serious problems to overcome.

First, if you do really obvious things like hitting toward the wrong green on a course you play regularly, or trying to cut off a dogleg with a 300-yard carry, or putting out of a pot bunker, your boss or that important client or whoever it is is going to catch on and be even madder at you than if you closed him out 10 and 8.

And second, it goes without saying that the only time you play really great golf is when you're doing your damnedest to play bad golf.

But over the years I've developed a few techniques that I have used with some success, most recently in a match against my I.R.S. auditor that I lost on the final hole when I somehow mistook a ball retriever for an 8-iron. Here are just a few:

- Leave the club-head cover on your driver when you tee off.
- Swing with your eyes shut.
- Play with a set of borrowed clubs and wear a left-handed gardening glove.
- Use brand-new balls on water holes and whenever out of bounds is on the right.
- When you're about a 5-iron from the pin, hit a hard 3-wood way over the green, then say you read the yardage on the sprinkler head upside down: It said 169, and you thought it was 691.
- Hit short shots crosshanded.
- Hold the putter with the same grip you'd use to screw two hoses together, and move your lips when you read the green.
- Talk in your own backswing.

· OUTCLUBBING YOUR ·
OPPONENT

With so many different brands on the market these days, it's pretty hard to know for sure which clubs are right for you, but convincing an opponent that his brand-new set of $1,500 graphite-shafted forged-steel irons and mumbo-jumbo woods is wrong for him is a piece of cake.

When someone I'm playing with shows up with a new set of sticks, I ask him to let me swing one, just to get the feel of it.

"Woo!" I exclaim, making a deliberately unbalanced swing that almost pulls me off my feet. "Did you have these clubs fitted?"

There's always the chance that he actually knows whether the shafts are regular or stiff, and where their kickpoint is, and what kind of swing weight they have, but even if he does, the seeds of doubt are sown.

"I don't know," I continue ominously, waggling the club back and forth with exaggerated care as if the head might fly off at any moment. "This thing has a mighty fast hostile moment, and the shaft has the stem torsion of a fireplace tool. I wonder if they used that obsolete counterclockwise-wound reverse-lay carbon-fiber matrix. The pros won't touch it. They call it 'Sclaffite,' because it makes you hit everything fat."

Then I take a close look at the back of the club head, tap it with a fingernail, and let out a low whistle. "Iridium alloy. They say it isn't toxic in small doses unless you have prolonged exposure, but, hey, is it worth the risk for a couple of extra yards?"

I flip it over and peer at the club face. "Y-shaped grooves," I say, clicking my tongue in disapproval. "Well, it's true they're technically legal until the end of next year. . . ."

I peer intently at the serial number on the club head. "That's peculiar," I remark with genuine surprise. "The serial number is odd (or even). I thought odd (or even) numbers were always reserved for women's clubs."

I hand him back the club.

"What's a set like that cost," I ask innocently. "Five, six hundred bucks?"

We haven't teed off on the first hole, and he's eighteen down.

· Match Play ·

You don't win golf matches by trying to take strokes off your score.

You win golf matches by doing everything within your power to see to it that your opponent adds strokes to his score.

· Habeas Golfballus ·

To me, the dumbest rule in golf is the penalty for a lost ball.

The fact is, when someone finds that nice, new two-dollar ball you sliced into the woods, he's not going to post a notice on the clubhouse bulletin board in an effort to return it to its rightful owner, is he?

Not on your life. He's going to keep it.

Therefore, a "lost" ball is actually a "stolen" ball, because although the theft will take place at some future date, it is absolutely inevitable that it will occur.

Now, it is bad enough that the perpetrator of this vile larceny both goes unpunished himself and gets to pocket the fruits of his unseemly crime, while the innocent victim of his transgression is unjustly punished by having to add a stroke he did not make to his score.

But this gross injustice is further compounded by a requirement that the golfer whose ball will have soon been plundered must put an additional "provisional" ball at risk of a second misappropriation.

The governing authorities of the game have already amply demonstrated that they cannot adequately police the golf course to prevent a recurrence of this criminal behavior, and stolen balls are openly and brazenly sold from bowls right out in plain sight in every pro shop in the land.

And yet these self-appointed guardians of golfing orthodoxy have the audacity, in the name of so-called "fair play," to require a golfer whose only offense was to hit a wayward shot to jeopardize his property once again.

Well, I say if the average law-abiding golfer cannot be protected against the predators who lurk along our fairways, then at least let him drop a ball without penalty in a secure, well-lighted part of the fairway adjacent to the scene of the foreordained crime and proceed with his lawful play.

Yes, he will be uncompensated for his loss, but at least he will not have to bear the heavy burden of an additional cruel and unnecessary punishment.

I rest my case.

· DRIVE FOR DOUGH ·

You've probably heard that familiar golf cliché "Drive for show, putt for dough."

I happen to think that driving is more important than putting, but I don't mean driving the ball, I mean driving the cart.

Why? First of all, whoever drives keeps score, since the scorecard and pencil are on a little clipboard thing in the middle of the steering wheel of the cart, and whoever keeps score has a significant advantage.

Second, as driver, you can—and should—always take your opponent over to his ball first, even if you're away, then get him to hurry his club selection by rocking the cart gently back and forth with a few light taps on the accelerator as he fumbles in his bag for the right stick. As soon as he picks one, immediately speed away—he's almost certain to feel he's got the wrong club.

When you stop by your own ball, line the cart up so that it blocks his view of your lie. If he's on the other side of the fairway, you're not going to be able to see him roll his ball into a perfect lie, but who cares? He's going to do it anyway, and more important, he's going to assume that you put *your* ball on an actual tee, and even if you don't, the idea that you might have will deeply annoy him.

Also, one of the best ways to take the wheels off a competitor's game is to propel him out of the passenger seat on a sharp curve somewhere early in the round. All it takes is a good full turn, and that's a lot easier to make when you're driving the cart than when you're driving a ball.

And finally, although scientists are at a loss to explain the phenomenon, it is an undeniable fact that the quicker you get to a ball that you sliced toward a water hazard or the out of bounds markers, the greater the odds that you will find it in a decent lie just short of the trouble. And this is especially true if your opponent is standing on the other side of the fairway, 150 yards from his bag strapped on the back of the cart, trying to figure out how to hit a 75-yard approach shot with a 5-wood.

· A STORY BY ·
BILL CLINTON

I remember early in the presidential campaign in 1992 I was out in Los Angeles on a fund-raising trip, and I was about to play a round of golf with a few of the fine folks in the film industry who were so generously supporting my candidacy.

I'd stuck a few new Titleists in my pocket, and I was headed for the practice green to try a new putter Hillary had bought for me, when who should walk up but Leslie Nielsen.

"Governor Clinton," he said to me affably, pointing to my pants. "What's that in your pocket?"

"Golf balls," I replied, a little puzzled by his question.

"Golf balls," he repeated, as if giving the matter a good deal of thought. "Tell me," he said finally, "is that anything like tennis elbow?"

· YOU COULD LOOK IT UP ·

I don't know why it is, but the only thing all golf instruction books have in common is the phrase "contrary to what most other teachers say . . ."

· A MATTER OF ·
SOME GRAVITY

If a putt goes right over the hole and doesn't drop in, or runs around the inside of the cup and comes back out again, is it in?

In other words, do the laws of gravity take precedence over the Rules of Golf?

I put that question to Dr. Kurt Fulcrum of the University of Zurich at Les Alpes, a distinguished gravity lawyer and a twenty-one handicapper on the challenging U.Z.L.A. course.

His reply was as succinct as it was colorful.

"Ach, Leslie," he said to me, "take zis simple test. Hold zee Rules of Golf in your arm-foot" (I think he meant hand) "and drop it. If it floats to zee ceiling, I will eat my head-glove" (I think he meant hat).

I once saw the U.Z.L.A. club champion let Fulcrum pick up a twenty-two-foot putt after a two-minute lecture on wormholes and the hidden curvatures of space, so believe me, he knows what he's talking about.

· How to Score ·

Golfers always complain that no matter how they're playing, they always seem to score even worse. They may be playing solid high-nineties golf, but they come back with a 118.

I can't put it any more simply than this: The way to score in golf is to score.

By that I mean you must *always* be the scorekeeper.

There is a very practical reason for this, as well as a psychological one.

The practical one is that as scorekeeper, you get to announce your score *second,* and this enormous advantage is absolutely critical to improving your score.

The psychological reason is subtler but no less compelling: As scorekeeper, you immediately assume a quasi-official status, making it harder for other players to challenge *your* score and forcing them to turn to you as the ultimate arbiter of the accounting of *their* scores.

Let's take a look at a few typical scoring situations and see how to master the fine art of turning three strokes into two, or one, or none.

Situation No. 1. Your opponent had a 6, and you had an 8 that would have been a 9 if your casual backhanded tap-in putt hadn't found the hole after bouncing off your foot.

Take the initiative. Say, "So what did you have there, a five?"

He will immediately accept this lower score. Remark a little grumpily that a 5 beats a 6 every day, and put down a 6 for yourself. Don't get greedy. You're not trying to win the hole at this point, you're just trying to stop the bleeding. (Later on, when you add up the score, you can turn that numeral "6" into a numeral "4" if you make those pencil strokes properly. Remember: sloppy writing can make up for sloppy play.)

Your opponent can't question your 6 without undermining his own 5. In the extremely unlikely event he says "No, I took a six on that hole," you are playing with a dangerous lunatic. Make this your last round with this certifiable nutcase.

Situation No. 2. He's on the green in 2, but he's a long way from the hole and isn't a strong putter. You lie 3 somewhere off the putting surface. You chip onto the green and end up closer to the hole, but nowhere near it—maybe twenty feet away. You now lie 4.

Walk right over, say "I guess I'm out of this hole," and pick up your ball, then go and tend the pin for his birdie putt. Put the heat on him with a little too much encouragement. Tell him he owes it to himself to make this putt. Urge him not to leave a birdie putt short. Remind him how unique an achievement a birdie would be.

If he makes it, give him his 3 and take a 4. If he misses the birdie, give him the 4, and take a 5. (Remember, later on, just as your "6" can become a

"4," his "4" can become a "6" and his "3" can become an "8.")

But if, as is much more likely, he three-putts, shake your head sadly and say, "Hey, what can you do, a pair of fives." Smother him in sympathy. Criticize the pin position. Blame spike marks on the green. Tell him he was robbed. After all, it's the truth.

Situation No. 3. This time you've got the upper hand. You lie 3 just short of the green. He hit a drive out of bounds, and then muffed his provisional, and hit a lousy approach shot. He's a bit closer to the hole, but he lies 5.

As you get ready to hit, ask him in an offhanded way, as if you're trying to decide how aggressive to be with your shot, "What do you lie, six?"

When he vehemently protests that he lies only 5, look surprised. When he starts angrily recounting his strokes, cut his narrative short with a generous but dismissive wave of the hand, adding, "No, no, whatever you say, five it is."

You are probably going to win this hole. But if disaster should strike, at the very least you've laid the groundwork to get an easy half, and if you do well and get down in 5 or even 6, and he holes out for a totally legitimate 7, you can add to the damage by saying in a kindly sort of way, "Why don't we give you a seven on that hole?" as if you were doing him a favor.

If his annoyance at your implicit accusation causes him to get an 8, insist on giving him a 7. Not only will this inexplicable bit of generosity (or is it veiled contempt?) further unnerve him, but the fact is it's a lot easier to turn a numeral "7" on the scorecard into a "9" than to do anything at all with an "8."

Situation No. 4. On this hole, each of you suffered a major detonation. You had a lost ball, sent a recovery shot out of bounds, and knocked a couple in the water. He slashed at the ball a half-dozen times in the deep rough, then shanked it into a fairway bunker and took three strokes to get out.

You've now both hit onto the green, and you each

putted once, and you're about the same distance from the hole, but you're away.

You lie 10. He lies 11 or 12. Who cares?

Line up your putt with great care, as if you were on one of those rare but challenging par-12s and you had a real shot at a birdie 11.

If the putt goes in, make a big hand-pumping victory move. If it doesn't, act like it really mattered.

Either way, give him his putt.

When you do this, he is bound to ask you what you got on the hole, and this is one of the few instances where you will appear to give your score first. You say "Slmnkt (this is hard to transliterate, but any inaudible one-syllable word will do) tuple bogey."

Your opponent knows you had at least a 12, so he will react with outrage at what sounded to him like a claim you had only a double bogey. No doubt he will accuse you of lying and cheating, and he'll probably insist you had at least a 10. He'd make it a higher figure, one closer to the truth, but he'll be hoping to negotiate his own score down to a 7.

React with astonishment and hurt to this outburst, then say, as if speaking to a child, "I said setuple bogey (or quintuple or sextuple) whatever, depending on the par of the hole, would make it a twelve.

"I gave you your putt for your octuple," you should add in a somewhat frosty tone.

That, of course, makes his score a 13, and costs him the hole, not to mention a major loss of face, but after his false accusation, he is in no position to argue.

To sum it all up, in golf, unlike poker, there is only one card—the scorecard. And if you have the scorecard, you're holding *all* the cards.

· Some Good Advice ·

The only advice I would ever give another golfer, which I would never actually give another golfer in any case because of my lifelong rule against ever giving anyone unsolicited advice, is never give another golfer unsolicited advice, including the advice to never give another golfer unsolicited advice.

· A Crazy Ruling ·

What do you do if your ball lands in a divot hole in the fairway that's been filled with that sand mixture they use during tournaments on fancy courses?

They made Ernie Els play his ball from just such a lie when that happened to him in a recent U.S. Open.

It's shocking that no U.S.G.A. official knew the appropriate rule to apply in this situation.

It's the rule on obstructions. Since the sand in the divot is clearly an "artificial surface," those sand-filled divots are in fact tiny little cart paths, and you get to drop the ball a club-length away.

The fact that tiny little carts are rarely observed using these apparently randomly constructed segments of unfinished roadway is, like so much else in the Rules of Golf, simply irrelevant.

· SECOND THINGS FIRST ·

On the first tee, a lot of players calm their nerves by letting everyone know right off the bat that if they make a lousy drive, they're going to hit another shot.

At the A.T.&T. Pro-Am at Pebble Beach, Jack Lemmon likes to drop a couple of extra balls on the back of the tee box just to make that point clear.

Now, I have nothing at all against taking Mulligans, and not just on the first tee, but also on par-5s, long par-4s where you're apt to overswing, shorter par-4s with doglegs or weird hazards that unfairly make you try to steer the ball, and par-3s, where it's easy to overdo it trying to get a hole in one.

Occasionally, however, you may find yourself in a high-stakes match where taking an otherwise perfectly acceptable Mulligan might be frowned upon.

The trick in these situations is to tell yourself to hit the *second* ball *first*.

True, it won't be as spectacular as the first one, but

since the do-over usually works out all right, it's bound to be a lot more playable than a ball banged deep into the woods.

Also, chances are you won't even need to hit the first ball at all, which gets you off the tee in a positive frame of mind and gives you a leg up on your fellow players who will never realize that your solid, respectable initial shot was, in fact, a Mulligan.

· THE POWER OF ·
POSITIVE PUTTING

Why can't I putt?

I can't tell you how often I've heard golfers ask themselves that question.

The reason is simple: lack of confidence. You must have total confidence in your putting in order to eliminate all the nervous shakes and jerks and twitches that spoil your touch and destroy your accuracy.

And what is the source of unshakable confidence? Sinking putts.

In other words, to putt well, you must *already* be putting well. To putt well today, you've got to putt well yesterday, and to putt well tomorrow, you must putt well today, because by tomorrow, today will be yesterday.

I know what you're going to say. The last thing I

need while I'm lining up a tricky little six-footer is even more pressure, but that is the way it is.

Wait, did you say, *six*-footer?

Pick that thing up. For Pete's sake, if a tap-in like that isn't a gimme, I'm a ham sandwich.

· DON'T QUIT ON ·
THE SHOT

There's a saying in golf that you don't hit the ball with your follow-through.

That may be the case when your shot goes a reasonable distance forward along level ground, but it certainly isn't true when you're chipping up a steep, closely mown slope toward an elevated green, or you're at the bottom of a deep bunker with a big overhanging lip.

In situations like that, you may have to hit a "follow-up" shot, and you need to make that second swipe at the ball a smooth and integral part of your initial swing.

What you want is a fluid, uninterrupted propeller-like motion of the club similar to those dopey practice swings you've probably seen some golfers take where they bring the club completely around and go right into another practice swing, almost without stopping.

Tempo is absolutely critical here. You're better off making two or three lazy, twirl-the-lariat loops to give the ball enough time to come back into range than stopping at the top with the club held like you were getting ready to kill a snake. What you're trying to do is make whatever lunge you have to take toward the ball to hit it as it rolls by seem like part of a natural, if somewhat pronounced, Gary Player–style forward shift of your weight into your final follow-through.

I would also hasten to add that while this "encore" shot is quite a pretty thing to see when properly executed, its success, sadly, is entirely dependent on the absence of an attentive audience.

· TAKING RELIEF ·

It should come as no surprise that it was the great Bobby Jones, who wrote with such eloquence and insight on every other aspect of the game of golf, who brought blessed lucidity to the often confusing subject of where, and when, to take relief.

He wrote: "No matter how great a sense of urgency he may feel in responding to a persistent and pressing call of Nature, a player should refrain from untrousering his apparatus until he has fully considered all the factors which may bear upon the business.

"Not the least of these concerns is the likelihood of the unheralded arrival upon the scene of a lady whose attendance at a display of extramural urination would surely serve to mortify even the least mannered of men.

"When the possibility of observation by a representative of the gentler sex has been satisfactorily excluded, the procedure to be followed is fairly straightforward, but here again undue haste is to be avoided. Even the arrangement of so simple an affair as selecting a venue for the accomplishment of the matter at hand that both affords adequate screening from public view and yet takes into account the prevailing wind may suffer from a too cursory consideration of the effects of a sudden change in its speed and direction.

"In this regard, it has been my experience that the minor inconvenience of making a short detour into the surrounding woods or shrubbery is well worth the modest expenditure of time and effort it entails, for not only has the individual seeking relief thereby assured himself of a high degree of privacy, but he has as well eliminated the deleterious effects of any wayward gusts or zephyrs upon the trajectory of his discharge.

"Now he has only to assume a stance of sufficient width to provide an ample margin for error in his aim, and see to it that his footing is level and secure, for it is well to bear in mind that once the process of draining the dew from one's lily has been commenced, it is not easily interrupted. Likewise, he should select a striking point for the dispersal of his stream such that whether it is a horizontal surface, like a rock or patch of bare ground, or a vertical one, like a tree, in neither case will he be at risk of besmirching his garments. Further, he should take care to ascertain that his piccolo has fully played its tune before it is replaced in his pants, for having announced an intention to go and see a man about a dog, it will be with no little embarrassment that a golfer returns from the interview looking as if the animal in question took it into his head to pee upon his leg."

· How to Add Fifty to · One Hundred Yards to Your Drive

More and more golfers are venturing out onto the links these days in what I consider pretty silly-looking outfits.

I suppose you could say it's all just a matter of personal taste, but it seems to me that if you're going to dress up in something that makes you look ridiculous, you might as well go the whole hog and wear a dress and a wig.

That way you can tee off from the ladies' tees, and let me tell you, when it comes to getting a little extra yardage on your drives, it's much better to *be* Big Bertha than to swing one.

· How to Miss Putts · Like a Pro

You really can't learn much from watching golf on television, other than how to pronounce Ballesteros's and Olazabal's names and who's endorsing Nike.

But there is one thing you can pick up from watching the top golfers play, and that is how to miss putts like a pro.

Since no one can ever putt worth a damn two days in a row, it's a very useful thing to know. Sure, you're still going to leave that 4-footer two feet short, and bang those 15-footers five yards past the hole, but you're going to look good doing it.

The first thing you absolutely have to master is ball marking. *Always mark your ball.* I don't care if you're away and you have a 40-foot putt that isn't in anybody's line, mark your ball and pick it up.

You can't repair spike marks in the path of your putt, but you can clear away little bits of leaves and pebbles and things like that. Even if there's nothing there, make a sweeping motion with your hand and toss some invisible piece of debris off the green. Look disgusted. Your thought here should be "What is this crap doing on a green in hallowed Amen corner at Augusta National in this, the final round of the Masters."

Crouch behind the hole and look back along your line. Resist the temptation to lie on your stomach and turn your head sideways so your eye is level with the ball. You're Corey Pavin, not Milton Berle.

Walk back and replace your ball, carefully aligning the logo with the hole. Step back, crouch again, and plumb-bob the putt by holding your putter like a pendulum and looking along the shaft. I don't know what you're supposed to see, but don't look puzzled. Compress your lips and make a brief nod, as if saying to yourself, "Double reverse break, about forty degrees into the grain, aiming point five balls above the cup, bent grass double cut and rolled to twelve on the Stimpmeter, a couple of three-eighths of an inch deep spike marks eleven and a half feet out, barometer about 29.85 and rising, market steady, long bond off ten basis points, soybeans weak, pork bellies firming."

Set up a little away from the ball. Take two identical practice putting swings, then move up, place the putter head in front of the ball, lift it, and place it in back. Look at the hole. Look back at the ball. Tap and *freeze.*

Even if you have obviously stubbed the putt, or it's clear from the sharp metallic "plink" sound that the thing is going to roll off the green, don't betray any doubt or disgust. A little restrained body English is in order. Your expression should be one of restrained anticipation: "This baby is going *in!*"

When it becomes apparent that at its point of closest approach to the cup the ball will still be a good five feet away, react with total disbelief. Think "What is this? I putted that same line in the practice round with By-yah-STAY-rohss and Oh-LAH-tha-ball, and it went in the center of the hole!"

As the ball flies past the cup, you can also slump to your knees and drop the putter, but I'd really save these theatrics for one of those rare cases where the ball is actually right by the hole for a split second, even if it is doing twenty-five mph at the time.

Go over to your ball. If it's still on the green, mark it, pick it up, and hold it in the tips of your fingers as if it were a dead mouse. You get paid ten thousand bucks a year to use these things, but really, you might want to consider an endorsement contract from another manufacturer.

If you putted the ball off the green, go get a wedge, and as you set up to hit, look up in the sky with a really pissed-off expression.

God, those blimps are noisy.

· BUNKER PLAY ·

Sand traps are the bad golfer's nemesis, and the reason for this sad state of affairs is that most high-handicappers are in the dark when it comes to understanding exactly what a sand wedge is supposed to do.

Put simply, the sand wedge, with its heavy curved sole, has been carefully designed to produce one of two specific shots: to move about six pounds of sand a yard or two forward in a fan-shaped dispersal pattern without touching your ball at all, or to clip your ball cleanly off the sand and send it approximately the distance of a well-hit 2- or 3-iron.

Since neither of these shots is particularly useful around the green, attempting the aptly named "explosion" shot with this club is a patent waste of time.

That's why I recommend a radically different method of getting out of bunkers: the hand wedge.

Stand outside the bunker and take two or three

very fast, almost wild, practice swings with your sand wedge, then warn your opponent that you have been blading a lot of sand shots lately. This should "brush him back" to the far side of the green.

Step into the bunker and take a conventional, fairly open stance, but since, as we will soon see, it's very important to really "get down to the ball" on this shot, dig your feet in very deeply (up to your socks if possible), bend your knees sharply, and choke way down on the club, gripping it *only* with your left hand. Rest your right hand loosely on the underside of the shaft.

Make a slow three-quarter backswing, then, as you begin your downswing, drop your right shoulder, take your right hand completely off the club, scoop up the ball and a handful of sand in your right palm, and as you continue swinging the club with your left hand, release the ball and the sand in an easy under-arm toss up and onto the green.

Once the ball leaves your right hand, bring it back

to the club and regrip it for a normal-looking fol-
lowing through.

If you find it difficult to perform this admittedly
complex part of the swing, or if your opponent is
watching a little more intently than you'd like, then
instead of moving your hand back onto the club,
duck your head abruptly and start furiously waving
an imaginary bee away from your right ear. Leave the
bunker hurriedly with additional slapping and swat-
ting movements with your right arm.

Hey, nice out!

· One from the Heart ·

I remember one year I was playing in the Bob Hope Classic in Palm Springs, and I was paired with a young professional player with a lot of promise who I'm going to call Tom Brown (I'm not going to use his real name because I can't remember it).

Tom played well from tee to green, but he couldn't sink a putt to save his life. Finally, on the seventh or eighth green, he turned to me and said, "Leslie, I'm desperate. I'm putting like a doofus. Have you got a tip for me, anything at all?"

Hey, we've all been there.

"Here, Tom," I said, feeling a little foolish since Tom wasn't his real name, "I want you to have this," and I handed him five bucks.

I wish you could have seen the look on his face.

Golf isn't just a mind game—sometimes it's a heart game too.

· MIND OVER MUFF ·

Let's say you hit a pretty good drive, but then you stepped up and hacked at it with a 5-iron that took a two-pound divot and moved the ball about fifteen yards.

Now, are you going to let that rotten shot spoil the hole for you and maybe even ruin your whole round?

Or are you going to use a little simple self-hypnosis to get that flub out of your mind forever, as if it never happened, so you can continue your game with a positive outlook on life?

Put that 5-iron away.

Step back, close your eyes, and take a deep breath.

Open your eyes.

Caramba! Look at the divot some thoughtless player left sitting in the middle of the fairway! That sucker is the size of a raccoon!

Honestly, the lack of consideration some golfers

show for the course and their fellow players. It's a disgrace.

It's a good thing there are some public-spirited individuals, such as yourself, who will take a few extra seconds to stop the cart, get out, and fix a mess like this.

Okey-dokey. Back you go, little fella, green side up, tamp that baby down with a little toe tap. *Voilà*. A job well done.

And looky here. That drive must have taken a couple of big last-minute bounces, because it's about fifteen yards farther than it looked from the tee.

Just think of it as karma, a tiny reward for a good deed. What goes around comes around.

Looks like a 6-iron. Hmmm. Something tells me to swing easy.

· Tempo Fugit ·

People often ask me, "Leslie, in your opinion"—
"Timing," I always answer—"what is the biggest
problem with most golfers' swings?"

· ROLL THE CAMERAS ·

As a professional actor with a long career in the motion picture industry, I can tell you that if you're going to videotape your swing, you owe it to yourself to do the job properly.

You'll probably watch the results hundreds of times, so make up your mind to go for a world-class production, and that means a top-notch cameraman, an award-winning cinematographer, a first-rate composer, and the services of a state-of-the-art soundstage.

But most of all, it means that you've got to decide right from the start that you aren't going to let your ego get in the way of the final product.

That's why I was very pleased and flattered that Arnold Palmer agreed to play the role of me in my own video, and I must say, even though he has no formal theatrical training, he really captured that very special mix of grace and power that has long been my trademark as a golfer.

· YOU-DA-JERK ·

It began with Tom Watson at Pebble Beach and rapidly spread to every professional tournament in the world—the single stupidest phrase in all of golf: "You-da-Man!"

If you must express your admiration for a magnificent shot, at least show a little creativity.

When John Daly hits one 320 yards down the middle, I say:

"O club well swung! O dimpled sphere clean struck!
Thou has the fairway well and truly split.
Thou standst astride the links colossus-like
And we, mere mortals on this hallowed turf,
Proclaim thy godlike golfing mastery!"

· INSENSITIVITY TRAINING ·

Face facts. Your golf game is lousy—and most likely always will be—your swing is ugly, and you probably look funny in golf clothes.

If this makes you feel at all defensive, then you are far too sensitive for your own good, and you should begin work at once on developing a much greater degree of insensitivity.

As something of an expert on the subject, I have observed that insensitive types fall into three basic categories:

(1) Naturally insensitive
(2) Self-taught
(3) Seminar-trained

Frankly, I prefer the third category, because as the seminar indoctrination progresses, you become aware that you are becoming unaware, until you finally reach the point where you are totally unaware that you are totally unaware.

It is this complete lack of awareness that helps us, the bad golfers, to finish our rounds of golf with our heads held high. If we have not enjoyed ourselves, we are unconscious of the fact, and thus we are likely to think that we had a good time.

Thanks to this crucial insensibility, our self-esteem is left intact, and we preserve for ourselves the most important thing in golf, the very life of the royal and ancient game—the freedom to be bad.

If after reading this far, you find yourself saying "Who gives a rat's patootie?" you have achieved an admirable level of insensitivity.

Go right out and tee off immediately.

· THE GAME OF LIFE ·

Everybody always says that the game of golf is a lot like life. I could not agree more. Here are just a couple of ways in which my lifetime in golf has helped me with the game of life. I think they can help you too.

- The next time you get stopped for speeding, tell the cop you'll take the one-stroke penalty and go back and drive by again, only this time nice and slow.

- When the doctor sits you down and says it's time to change your lifestyle—start exercising more, lose thirty-five pounds, and cut out the steaks and martinis—try asking him if it's okay if, instead, you just changed your grip.

- And if you find yourself cornered by a bore at a party, and you can't figure out how to extricate yourself, just take out a sand wedge, open your stance, and play a good hard punch shot from just in front of your right heel.

· THE FOUR FORBIDDEN · WORDS OF GOLF

There are four words you should never utter on a golf course.

I'm not talking about "choke," "shank," "clutch," or "yips."

The words are "That's not my ball."

· A THOUGHT ·

If mastering the golf swing is really nothing more than a matter of developing the muscle memory necessary to perform an unfamiliar physical movement like, say, riding a bicycle, then why aren't there 7,500 books on how to ride a bicycle?

· Stop Me If You've ·
Heard This

There are exactly ten golf jokes, and everyone has heard them a million times, but that doesn't prevent the wacky laugh-a-minute life-of-the-foursome from making it a million and one.

I've found that the best defense against the course clown is a good offense. As soon as I see Mr. Comedy coming, I slip on a black armband and put on a long face.

When he asks what I'm in mourning for, I shake my head sadly and recount this terrible story.

"Just last week an old friend of mine was playing golf with his brother and sister-in-law. His brother shanked a one-iron, killing his wife instantly, then in his follow-through he was struck by lightning and died on the spot. My friend managed to drag their bodies to his condo, which fortunately was right there beside that hole. When he got there, he found his own wife in bed with the golf pro, and he shot them both dead. The shock of it all drove him crazy, and now he can't decide whether he's Jesus Christ or Arnold Palmer.

"I went to see him in the loony bin last week, but he was so far gone he didn't even recognize me," I conclude solemnly, barely suppressing a sob. "Poor guy—he thought I was a mermaid."

· If I Ran a Resort ·

It's a pleasure to be able to play golf in the winter in some warm place, but the way a lot of resort courses are run could use a little improvement.

For one thing, all too many of them have this stupid requirement that you keep the carts on the cart paths, so you always have to lug an armload of clubs back and forth across the fairway, and when you get to your ball, you still don't have the right club, and you know at some point you're going to leave a 6-iron out there and have to drive back and look for it.

To avoid this, I'd put the cart path right in the middle of the fairway, and if your ball goes way right into the cactuses or rocks or marshes, then a ranger should come out and bring it back, and apologize for the inconvenience.

Also, all the par-3s would have parallel "passing" holes where you could get by those snail-paced holi-

119

day foursomes out for a leisurely six-hour round, and all the places on the course where you can cut in front of someone would be clearly marked.

And if there are any trees or tall bushes in the way of a reasonable shot on a hole, they would be in those big tubs with wheels on them you see in hotel lobbies so if you got an unfair bounce and landed behind one, you could move it a little.

Water hazards are a scenic feature on courses, but they would be a lot more scenic—and the occasional wayward shot that landed in one would be easier to take—if they were made available on a regular basis to the local high schools for girls' swimming team practice, or if arrangements were made with the resort's shops to have fashion shows with scantily clad ladies modeling beachwear during peak playing hours.

I'd like to see all the par-5s, and maybe the long par-4s, built in a kind of valley or "pipeline" shape, with steep sides that sloped up so if your tee shot or fairway wood happened to stray to the left or right, you'd have a pretty good chance of getting a fair bounce. And I think all the yardages on the sprinkler heads should be about fifteen yards longer than the distances actually are, so you'd feel as though you were really whacking those second and third shots.

It has often occurred to me when I've been warming up on the practice putting green waiting to be called to the first tee over the P.A. system (it would be much classier if they used individual beepers) that it's really silly to have only one cup on the green when there are so many different ways to play the hole. I'd prefer to have a minimum of three separate holes on each green on the course so everyone had at least a fair shot at two-putting. And just as an added bonus, I'd make the holes six inches in diameter.

Did I mention that established movie stars and other world-class celebrities should always play free?

Well, that's just good public relations and plain old common sense.

· A MYSTERY ·

What is it about golf?

You watch Michael Jordan defy gravity as he scores a game-winning three-pointer, and you don't believe for one second that you could make that play.

And you don't think that you could ever hit like Ken Griffey, Jr., or pass like Phil Simms, or skate like Wayne Gretzky.

But you watch Nick Price stroke a nifty 6-iron stiff to the pin from 190 yards out, and you say to yourself, hey, if I just had a little more time to practice, and I smoothed out my swing and got my timing down, *I* could do that.

What can we learn from this?

Not much really, except it does explain why there aren't any miniature basketball courts along the highway, and no one is selling pink and green baseball uniforms, x-out footballs, and funny headcovers for hockey sticks.

· COURTESY FIRST ·

If you've got a bad lie in the fairway and you think there's a pretty fair chance you're going to flub the shot and take a big divot and then be so mad you're going to stomp off without replacing it, then I think you really owe it to the other players on the course to tee up your ball before you hit it.

· WHY CAN'T I PLAY LIKE · GREG NORMAN?

When you're watching a major golf tournament, don't you often wonder what separates the pros from the rest of us?

How is it possible, you ask yourself, for a human being to reach a 520-yard par-5 with a 340-yard drive and a 180-yard 9-iron, or hit a 2-iron out of deep rough stiff to the pin, or float a ball out of downhill fried-egg lie in a steep-sided bunker and spin it back inches from the hole?

The answer, of course, is that there is simply no way a human being can do any of those things. Professional golfers are space aliens from some distant galaxy. It's just a lucky accident that they'd rather play golf than enslave us, vaporize our cities, and have their hideous way with our womenfolk.

· THOSE SPECIAL ·
MOMENTS

Sooner or later, any golf writer worth his salt ends up waxing poetic about the mystical qualifies of the game and its strange hold on those who play it.

What golfer's heart doesn't beat a little faster as he remembers the time when, on a mere whim, he stopped at a golf shop along the highway in an unfamiliar city and found a $1,200 set of clubs he had long coveted in the pro shop of his own home course on sale for $699?

Who hasn't gone to the first tee with a little extra spring in his step, even at six-thirty in the morning, thrilled by the knowledge that the guy who edged him out of a parking space right by the bag drop has left his lights on?

And who can forget that sweet feeling of elation that comes over you as you discover that a member of that super-slow foursome in front of you that won't let you play through has left his sand wedge on the edge of the green, just a few short yards from the largest water hazard on the course?

Yes, there is a spiritual side to the game of golf.

· The Man in the · Mirror

When all is said and done, golf is not a competition between you and your opponent, or a test of your skill versus the course.

Golf is a struggle against yourself.

As you battle to master your emotions, overcome your natural instincts, conquer your fears, and wrestle your conscience to the ground, you will find yourself locked in a fight to the finish with the toughest antagonist you will ever encounter: you.

This is no average adversary. Here is a perfectly matched foe who is privy to your innermost thoughts, who anticipates your every move, and parries your every thrust.

And if you persevere, and get the better of yourself, the bitter price of your victory is the certainty of your own defeat.

Are you more than a match for yourself? Do

you have what it takes to bring yourself to your knees?

There's only one way to find out.

Plaaaaaaaaaay golf! And may the best man win!

· When to Take Up · Golf

What's the best time to take up golf?

I don't care if you're fifteen or fifty, the answer is still the same.

Ten years ago.

· Epilogue: ·

IF YOU PLAY BAD GOLF
YOU'RE MY FRIEND

People often say you can tell a lot about a person by the way he behaves on a golf course. I'm not so sure that's always true.

I remember in 1949 I had a part in a movie being filmed in Hong Kong—it was either *Dark Wind over China* or *Bamboo Boogie-Woogie,* I don't recall which —and on a lark, my stand-in, Ken Vils, and I went off to Canton, in what was soon to become the People's Republic of China, for the weekend. It was a kind of nutty thing to do, but we were young, and it beat playing mah-jonng with the wardrobe lady.

They had an eighteen-hole course just outside town that had been built by the British back in colonial days. It was in pretty bad shape, what with the Japanese occupation and the civil war, but the club

129

was open, so we paid our greens fees and headed out to the first tee.

No sooner had we pulled out our drivers when up come these two Chinese gentlemen in a battered jeep with a couple of sets of clubs strapped in back and a soldier in the middle standing by a .50-caliber machine gun on a swivel mount.

For all Ken and I knew, they were a pair of warlords or bandits or something, but these guys looked very friendly and cheerful. They motioned us to put our bags on the back, and so we figured, what the hell, and we made a foursome of it.

We're about to tee off, when a column of tanks rumbles up followed by a full infantry battalion—about five hundred really serious-looking soldiers with fixed bayonets. They line up along both sides of the first hole, and the guy who is obviously the commander comes up and salutes the two Chinese.

I look at Ken, and Ken looks at me, and then it hits me. We're paired with Mao Tse-tung and Chou En-lai!

Well, Mao has this kind of choppy, lift-and-drop, self-taught Sunday-hacker swing, and Chou, who has a gimpy right hand from some kind of war wound, has a sort of Raymond Floyd move, where he brings the club back way inside and does a little loop at the top. You knew that neither of them could break one hundred on a good day, but I've got to tell you, you couldn't find two players with nicer dispositions on any golf course in the world—always laughing, never a temper tantrum even when they hit terrible shots, and unfailingly polite and considerate.

Anyway, that's not really the point of the story. What I recall most vividly about the day was that Mao carried around this little red notebook, and every time something occurred to him, he'd jot it down. The only one I remember is "Power grows out of the handle of the club," which I took to mean that it was important to have a strong grip.

But when I got back home and took up the game in earnest, I remembered Mao's little red book, and I resolved to keep a journal of my own thoughts and reflections on the game.

And that is how you come to be holding this book in your hand. No, it isn't red—some other guy who must have played with Mao way back when beat me to it—but it is little.

And I can assure you, it is every bit as stupid as this story.

Latin For All Occasions
Henry Beard

Who says Latin is a dead language? The Roman mass may be a thing of the past, but Latin's never been livelier.

Henry Beard, former prisoner of the classics, has produced an essential tool for anyone who's ever struggled with an ablative. Here, in one handy volume, are hundreds of everyday English expressions rendered into grammatically accurate, idiomatically correct, classical Latin and an easy to use pronunciation guide.

Latin For All Occasions gives you the perfect phrase for every contemporary situation, from starting a relationship (*'Frequentasne hunc locum?'* – 'Do you come here often?') to making a swift exit (*'Di! Ecce hora! Uxor mea me necabit!'* – 'God! Look at the time! My wife will kill me!')

'Humour book of the year'   *The Times*

0 00 255383 X

Latin For
Even More Occasions
Henry Beard

The sequel to the highly acclaimed *Latin For All Occasions* is filled with even more essential Latin phrases for all those who share Henry Beard's mission to drag Latin into the twentieth century.

You can impress your friends as never before with your impersonations of Marlon Brando (*'Proeliator fuissem'* – 'I could've been a contender') and James Cagney (*'Tu, rattus turpis!'* – 'You dirty rat!'), breeze by maître d's with confidence (*'Cauponas percenseo'* – 'I'm a restaurant reviewer') and be the life and sole of the office party (*'Estne volumen in toga, an solum tibi libet me videre?'* – 'Is that a scroll in your pocket or are you just pleased to see me?')

Your Latin education simply isn't complete without it.

0 00 255134 9

The Official *Exceptions* to the Rules of Golf

Henry Beard

Finally, a rule book that lets you play golf *your* way.

Gathered here for the first time in one handy volume are the 46 time-honoured exceptions to the rules of golf, guaranteed to improve your game, including:

- ball swung at and missed (practice swing) – no penalty
- unnecessary rough – free kick
- punitive pin placement (impossible putt) – free practice putt
- cruel and unnecessary hazards (hell holes) – no penalty

This essential guide for all golfers also features appendixes to cover every eventuality, such as 'Course or Player in Substandard Condition', 'Adverse Weather' (winter rules), 'Unofficial Play' (twilight rules) and the all-important 'Basic Techniques for Improving Your Lie'.

No serious golfer should be without it.

0 586 21843 2

French for Cats
All the French your cat will ever need

Henri de la Barbe
(Henry Beard)

When one considers the characteristics of most cats – their gourmet love of food, their personal vanity, their haughty demeanour – it becomes obvious that French is simply their natural language.

Now, with this book, your cat can master such phrases as *'Je ne veux pas être châtré'* ('I do not want to be neutered') and *'Je veux qu'on remplisse mon bol immédiatement'* ('I want food in my bowl, now'), before moving on to more serious cosmic concepts such as *'Je ne veux pas faire le Grand Somme avant que mes neuf vies soient épuisées'* ('I do not want to take the Big Nap before my nine lives are up').

Charmingly illustrated throughout, *French for Cats* is a must for all lingusitically ambitious felines – and their owners.

ISBN 0 00 637823 4